INDIANS
of the
PLAINS

Troll Associates

INDIANS
of the
PLAINS

by Rae Bains

Illustrated by Robert Baxter

Troll Associates

Library of Congress Cataloging in Publication Data

Bains, Rae.
　　Indians of the Plains.

　　Summary: Describes the history, customs, people, and
day-to-day life of the various Indian tribes that lived on
the broad prairie lands between the Mississippi River
and the Rocky Mountains.
　　1. Indians of North America—Great Plains—Juvenile
literature. [1. Indians of North America—Great Plains]
I. Baxter, Robert, 1930-　　ill.　II. Title.
E78.G73B35　　1984　　978'.00497　　84-2645
ISBN 0-8167-0188-1 (lib. bdg.)
ISBN 0-8167-0189-X (pbk.)

One popular image of the American Indian shows a young brave dressed in a beaded vest, buckskin leggings, and a huge feathered war bonnet. He is riding a horse toward a herd of buffalo and carrying a spear or a bow and arrow.

This image may not be true of all Indians of the North American continent, but it is an accurate picture of the Plains Indians who lived in the broad prairie lands between the Mississippi River and the Rocky Mountains.

Most of the tribes that lived in the Plains, including the Crow, Sioux, Blackfoot, Pawnee, Cheyenne, Arapaho, and Comanche, were nomadic. That is they did not have permanent homes. They wandered from place to place, carrying their homes, called teepees, with them. But until horses were brought to North America by Europeans, the Plains Indians did not wander great distances from their home region.

Until horses were used, everything had to be carried by the people of the tribe or pulled by dogs. Two poles were tied to a dog's back. The ends of the poles were left to be dragged on the ground behind the dog.

Between the poles the Indians attached a rack made of sticks. Then they piled their belongings on the rack. This kind of sledge, called a travois, might also carry a baby in a cradle or a young child on top of the family's belongings.

Once the Plains Indians began to use horses, their way of life underwent a great change. The horse could pull a much heavier load on a travois than a dog could, and it could carry an Indian on its back. Mounted on horseback, the Plains Indians did not have to walk when they went hunting, when they moved their villages, or when they waged war. The distance they could travel increased greatly.

A few of the Plains tribes, such as the Mandans, were not nomadic. They lived in permanent, dome-shaped lodges. These were covered with thatch and turf, the top layer of the soil being held together by grass and roots.

The Mandans were primarily farmers, who raised grain and corn. They hunted buffalo, as the other Plains Indians did, but they hunted near their homes and did not stray from their village for long periods of time.

The majority of Plains Indians, however, were not farmers. Their lives centered around the hunt for buffalo. The massive, shaggy beast was the source of most of the food, clothing, tools, housing, and cooking implements of the Plains Indians.

Buffalo meat was either eaten fresh or preserved for use later on. Sometimes it was

boiled in a stew, and sometimes it was roasted over an open fire.

Buffalo meat that was to be preserved was cut into strips and dried on a rack. It could be eaten that way or pounded into a pulp and mixed with fat and berries. This pounded mixture was called pemmican.

The Plains Indians also hunted elk, wolves, grizzly bears, and antelope for their hides and meat. To this diet the Indians added berries, cherries, and wild turnips.

Every part of the buffalo was used by the Plains Indians. The skin was made into clothing, footwear, bedding, and teepees.

The women of the tribe made all the clothing and teepees. First, they had to prepare a skin. One way was to scrape off all the hair, then dry it in the sun, so that it became rawhide. Rawhide was rough and hard, but it made long-lasting moccasins and teepees.

The teepee of the Plains Indian had a framework of cedar or pine poles, each about twenty feet long. The tops of the poles were lashed together to form a cone-shaped frame.

A covering of buffalo rawhide was put over the frame. It took twenty or more hides, sewn together, to make one teepee cover.

The women of the tribe helped each other to make the cover. When it was completed, it and everything inside the teepee belonged to the woman who lived in it.

The inside and the outside of the teepee were decorated with paintings. The outside pictures showed buffalo, deer, and braves hunting on horseback or on foot. They showed tribal legends or enemies being slain. The paintings on the inside of the teepee were geometric shapes—stars, squares, triangles, circles, and diamonds.

The teepee cover did not reach to the very top of the poles. The opening at the top let the smoke from the cooking fire escape into the air. The door of the teepee was a leather curtain or circle of buffalo hide. There was no furniture inside, just bedding made of a pad of grass with an animal-skin cover.

The teepees were very practical. They were easy to carry when the tribe moved, little trouble to put up, warm in the winter, and cool in the summer.

The rawhide that was fine for making a
teepee, however, was too rough to be used for
clothing. So the women of the Plains tribes
also tanned some buffalo skins. To do this,

they scraped the hide clean with a tool made from a buffalo bone. Then they tied the hide to a frame made of poles. After that, a paste was prepared from buffalo liver, fat, and brains and rubbed into the hide to soften it.

The next step was to soak the buffalo skin in water, wring it out, and put it back on the frame. The final step was to rub, pull, and work the skin until it was very soft and smooth all over. Then it would be sewn into leggings, shirts, skirts, and other kinds of clothing. Sometimes, the hair was left on a tanned hide. This made a warm winter robe or blanket.

The clothing of the Plains Indians was decorated with softened, painted porcupine quills and beadwork. Until the Indians acquired glass and porcelain beads in trade with the settlers, they made beads from berries, stones, animal teeth, and horns. The designs of the beadwork were geometric, like the paintings inside the teepee.

Buckskin fringes were another form of clothing decoration. Geometric designs were also painted onto robes and shirts worn by the braves. The paints were made from berries and colored earth.

The women of the Plains tribes dressed in moccasins, leggings, and loose dresses. A typical dress was made of two tanned elk skins, one for the front and one for the back. Over the dress was worn a short cape and a belt around the waist. The cape and belt were ornamented with beads, porcupine quills, or elk teeth.

In most Plains tribes both men and women wore their hair long, either braiding it or letting it hang loose. Some tribes had special ways of wearing their hair. For example, the Pawnees shaved their heads, except for a strip of hair that ran from the forehead to the back of the neck.

Among some of the tribes, the braves wore one or more eagle feathers in their hair. The number of feathers, the way they were worn, and how they were cut or painted told something about the wearer.

A feather that sloped toward the back meant that the brave had received a wound in battle. A feather split at the end meant that the brave had suffered many wounds. A dot on the feather meant that a brave had killed an enemy. And a notched red feather meant that the brave had taken a scalp.

War bonnets were worn only by great and respected chiefs. A war bonnet was made of a buckskin cap, to which a long strip of hide

was sewn. The two trailing ends of the hide were decorated with eagle feathers. The greater the chief, the more feathers on his cap. The greatest chiefs among the Plains Indians also wore buffalo horns attached to their war bonnets.

The animal-skin shirt, leggings, and robes of the men were worn only in cold weather or on ceremonial occasions. Usually, the men wore nothing more than a breechclout and moccasins. But the men made a great effort to have well-made bows and arrows, lances, war clubs, and other hunting and fighting implements. Hunting skills and bravery ranked very high in the life of the Plains Indians.

The bravest deed of all in battle was to touch a live enemy with a coup stick. A coup stick was a short piece of wood carried by warriors in battle. Stealing an enemy's horse was also a deed of valor and was another form of coup. For each coup a Plains Indian added to his credit, he was entitled to wear an eagle feather.

Bravery and the ability to withstand hardship and pain were important to the Plains Indians. This was true not only in battle but at tribal ceremonies and festivals. Every year a Plains tribe met to hold a festival called the Sun Dance. It was one of the highlights of the year for the whole tribe.

The Sun Dance festival lasted about twelve days. The first four days were for traveling and setting up teepees. The next four days were called the "Getting Ready Time." During this time the ceremonial lodge was built, feasts were held, and there were games and competitions for all—men, women, and children.

The final four days were devoted to the Sun Dance itself. In the Sun Dance the warriors danced around the center pole of the lodge for hours and hours. As they danced they stuck sharp sticks into their skin. Though they bled and suffered intense pain and exhaustion, the dancing braves refused to show any distress. The scars left by the sticks were worn as badges of honor for the rest of their lives.

The free, nomadic life of the Plains Indian ended in the middle of the nineteenth century. The land, which they had roamed for so long, was taken over by the settlers. The railroad—the hated "iron horse"—cut through the old hunting territories. The buffalo herds, which once numbered as many as fifty million buffalo, were slaughtered until they were nearly extinct.

Like the buffalo, the Plains Indians were victims of forces beyond their control. Some of them fought back, some moved farther west, and some moved onto reservations. Today, little remains of the traditional lifestyle of the Indians of the American Plains—but their proud and colorful history lives on.